Mrs.

ed emberley's

PICTURE PIE 2

a drawing book and stencil

LITTLE, BROWN AND COMPANY   BOSTON   NEW YORK   TORONTO   LONDON

the idea

PICTURE PIE 2 uses these 2 shapes ■ ● divided like this: ◨ ◕ to make things like this:

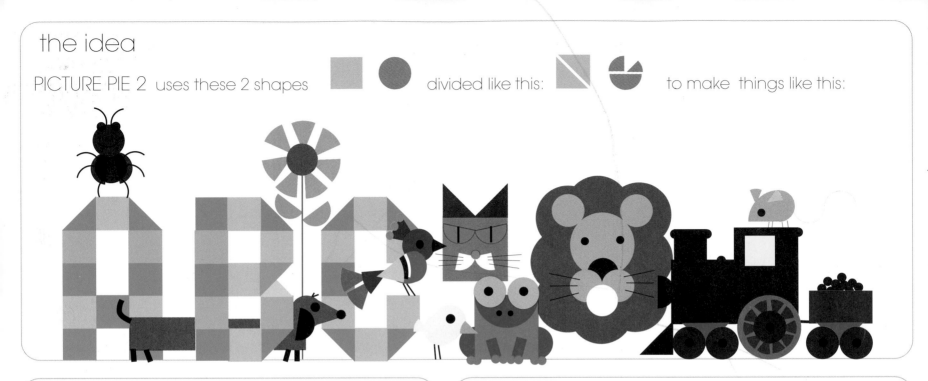

the stencil
A stencil is included to help you draw the shapes and lines.

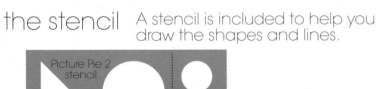

Picture Pie 2 stencil

L   M

● XS

Use these three shapes to make small letters

S   S   M

what, where

Step-by-step instructions show:
1. which shape to use   2. its color
3. its size, and   4. where to place it.

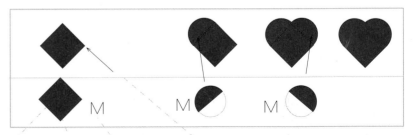

M   M   M

1. square 2. red 3. medium 4. Place as shown.

tools and materials

Other than this book and the stencil, you will need:

a pencil

scissors

glue

paper or other materials such as construction paper, origami paper, wallpaper, wrapping paper, felt, or cloth.

cut and paste

The step-by-step instructions in this book use a cut-and-paste method:

Draw shape.

Cut it out.

Apply glue.

Stick it down.

for inquiring minds...

see the last few pages of this book to find out more about:

how to use this book working with colored pencils or paints

how to make and use your own templates to create other size shapes

how to replace a lost or damaged stencil

The stencil will make a bluebird this size,

bluebird

a flower this size,

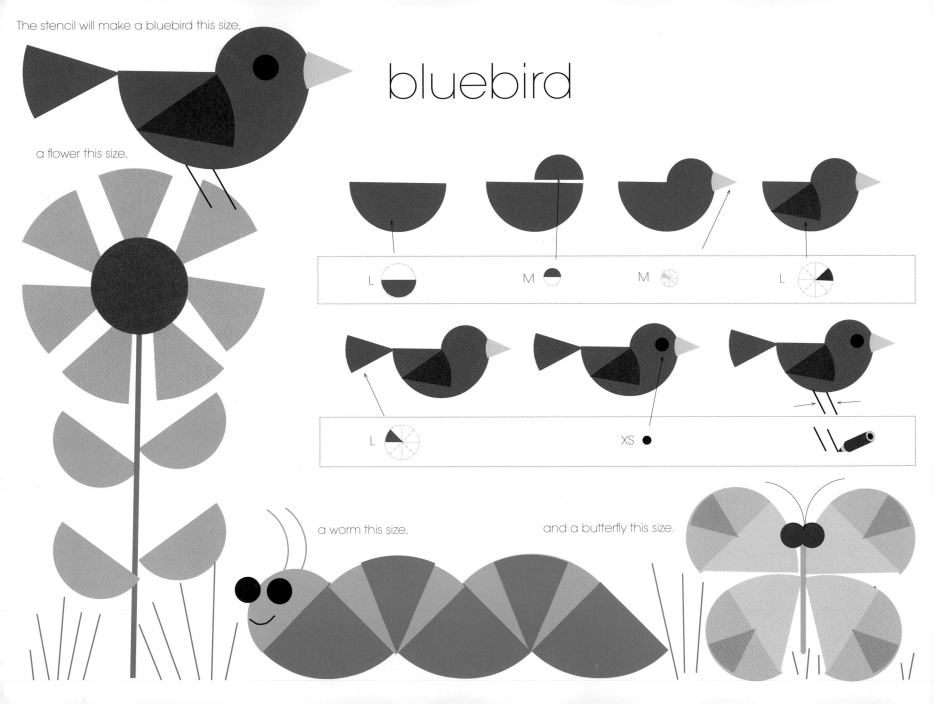

| L | M | M | L |

| L | XS ● | |

a worm this size,

and a butterfly this size.

butterfly

L · · L · · · M ○○○○ M ○○○○ XS ●● M ○●

flower

M ● M ○○ L ○ Make 7. M ●

worm

L ○○○ L ○○ M ○ L ○○

XS ● XS ● L ○○

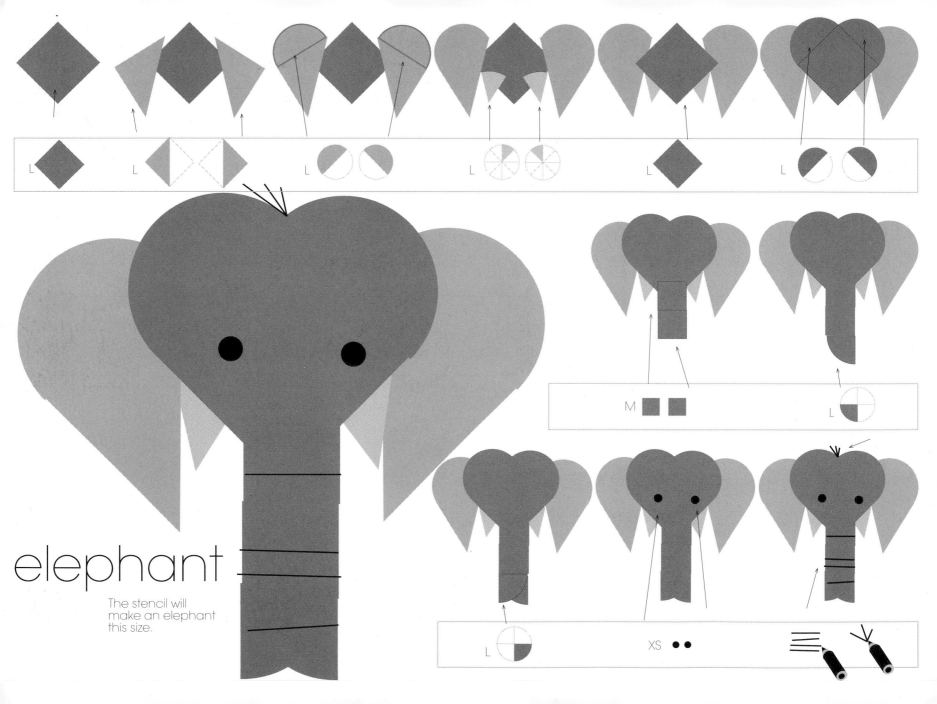

elephant

The stencil will
make an elephant
this size.

L

L

L

L

L

L

M

L

L

XS

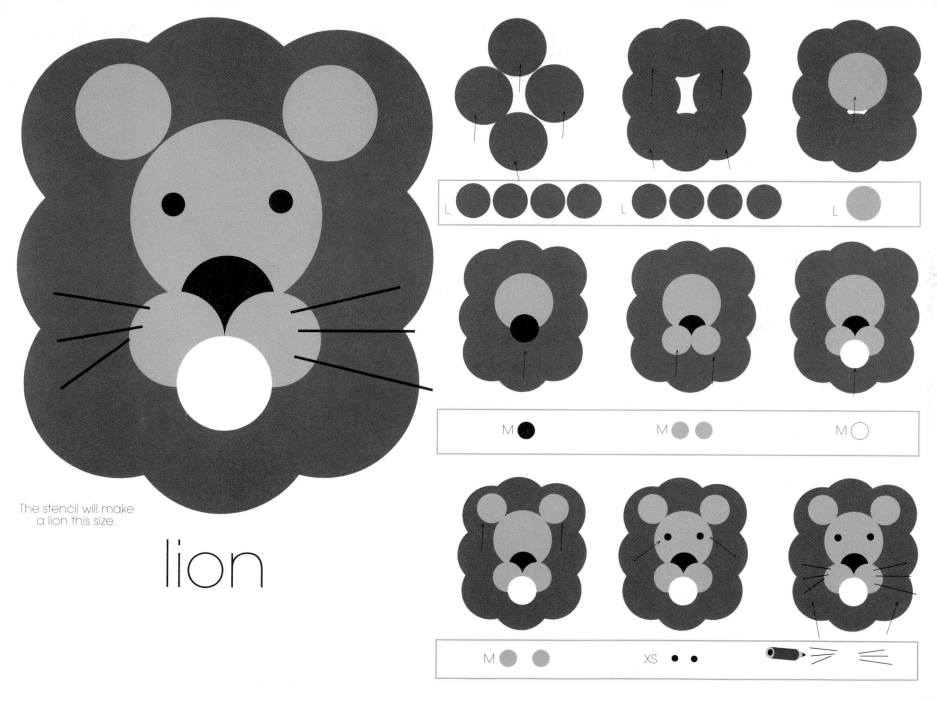

The stencil will make
a lion this size.

lion

L ● ● ● ● ●   L ● ● ● ● ●   L ●

M ●   M ● ●   M ○

M ● ●   XS • •

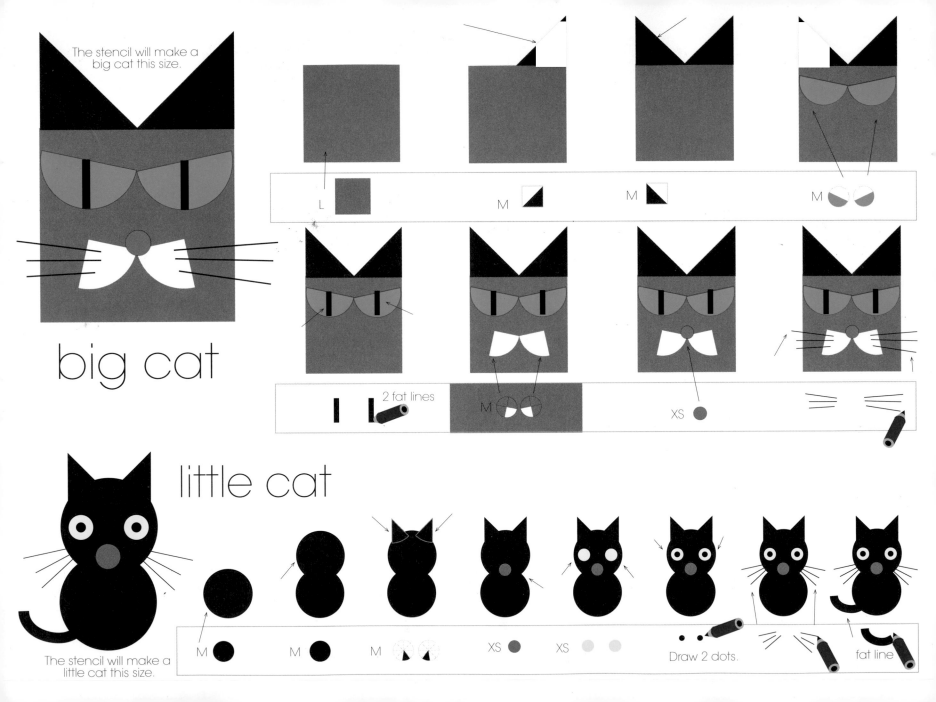

The stencil will make a
big cat this size.

big cat

L

M

M

M

2 fat lines

M

XS

little cat

The stencil will make a
little cat this size.

M

M

M

XS

XS

Draw 2 dots.

fat line

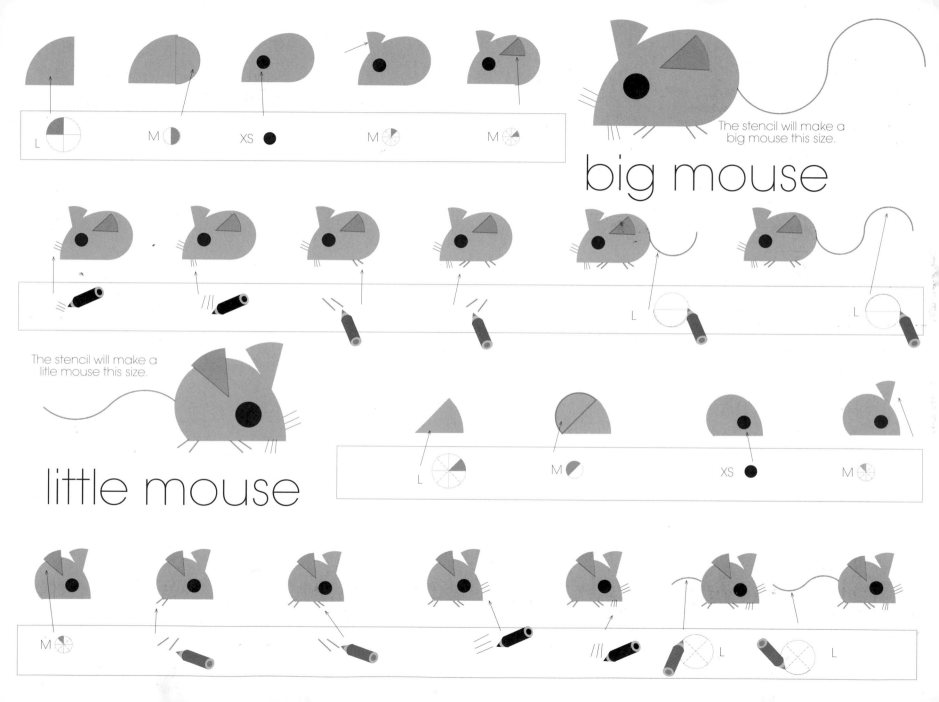

The stencil will make a
big mouse this size.

big mouse

The stencil will make a
litle mouse this size.

little mouse

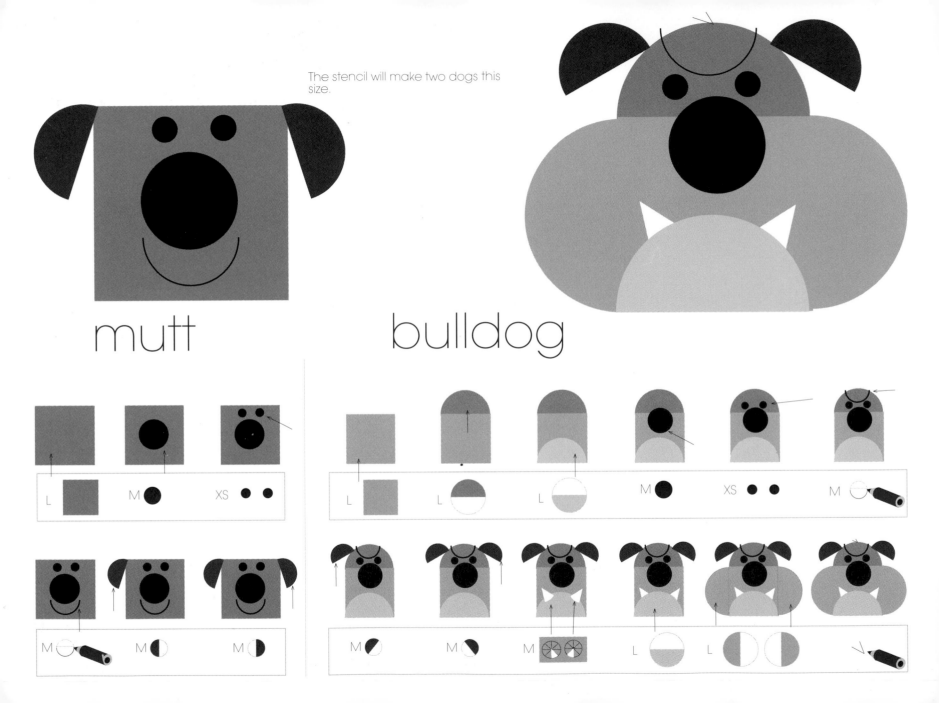

The stencil will make two dogs this size.

mutt

bulldog

L M XS

M M M

L L L M XS M

M M M L L

long dog

The stencil will make a dog this size.

M ▪ ▪ ▪ ▪

M ●

L ⊕

M ◑

XS ●

XS ●

rabbit

frog

The stencil will make a frog this size.

M ●●   XS ●●   Draw 2 dots.

L ■   L ◑

M ◐ ◑   XS ●● ●●   XS ●●●●

winking frog

The stencil will make a rabbit this size.

L ●   M ○   M ●●   XS ●●   L   L ◐ ◑   XS ●●●   S

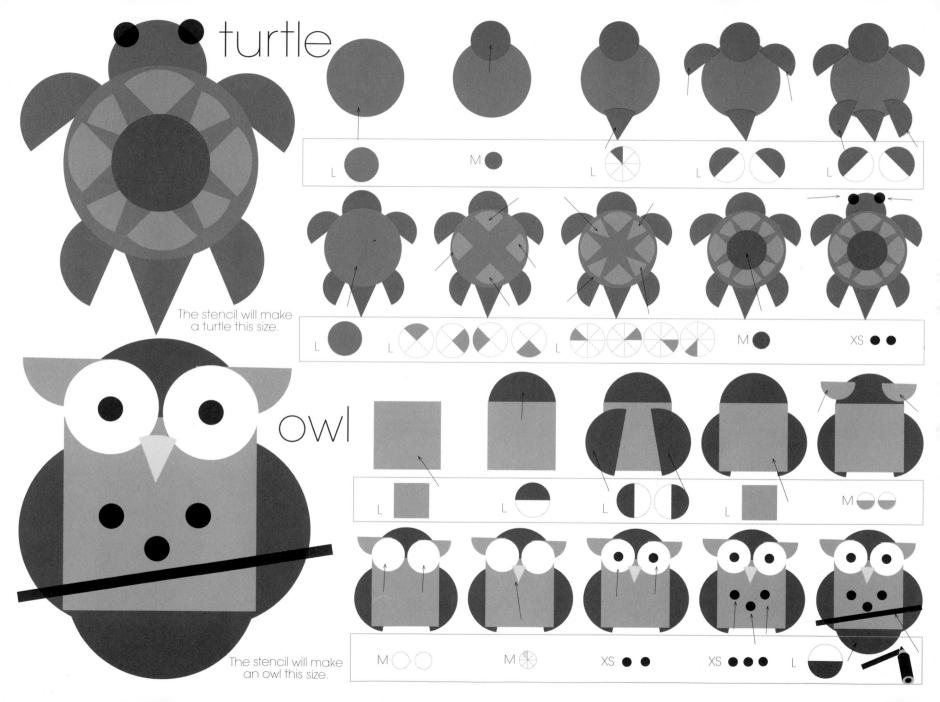

turtle

The stencil will make a turtle this size.

L ●   M ●   L ⊗   L ◐◑   L ◖◗

L ●   L ◔◕◔◕   L ◓◒◓◒   M ●   XS ●●

owl

The stencil will make an owl this size.

L ▮   L ◐   L ◑◑   L ▮   M ▬▬

M ○·   M ⊗   XS ●●   XS ●●●   L ◒

polar bear

The stencil will make
a polar bear this size.

L   M   L

L   M   XS   M

L   L   L   M   M

XS   M   M   M

penguin

The stencil will make
a penguin this size.

sea bird

The stencil will make a sea bird this size.

L

L

L

L

M

M

XS

seal

The stencil will make a seal this size.

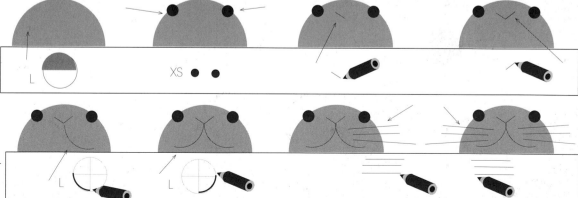

L

XS

L

L

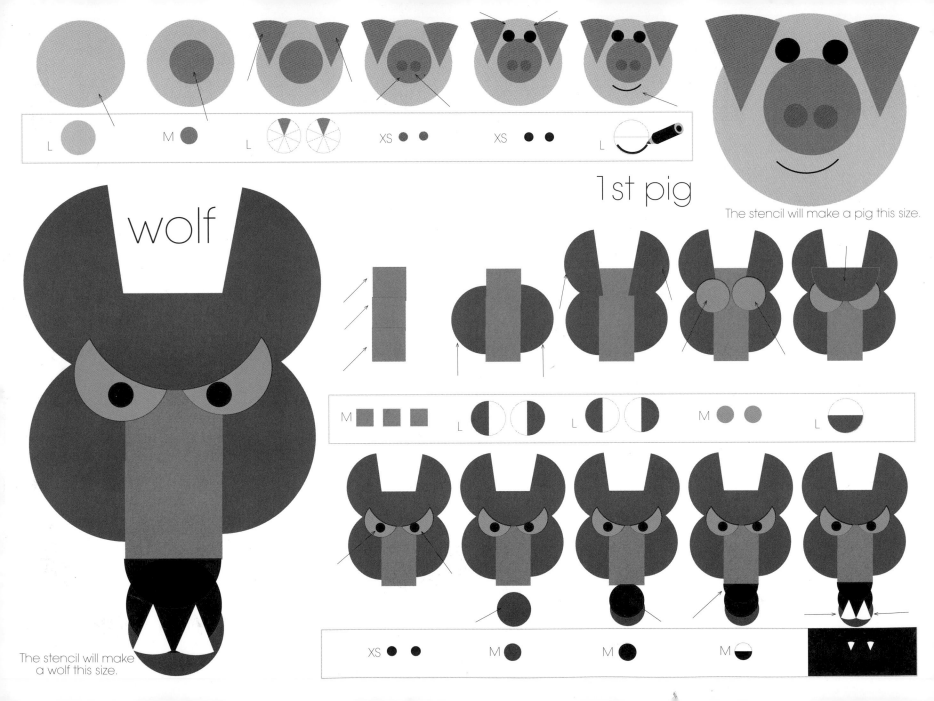

wolf

1st pig

The stencil will make a pig this size.

M   L   L   XS   XS   L

M   L   L   M   L

XS   M   M   M

The stencil will make
a wolf this size.

L   M   L   XS   XS   L

2nd pig

The stencil will make
a bigger pig this size.

3rd pig

The stencil will make
an even bigger pig this size.

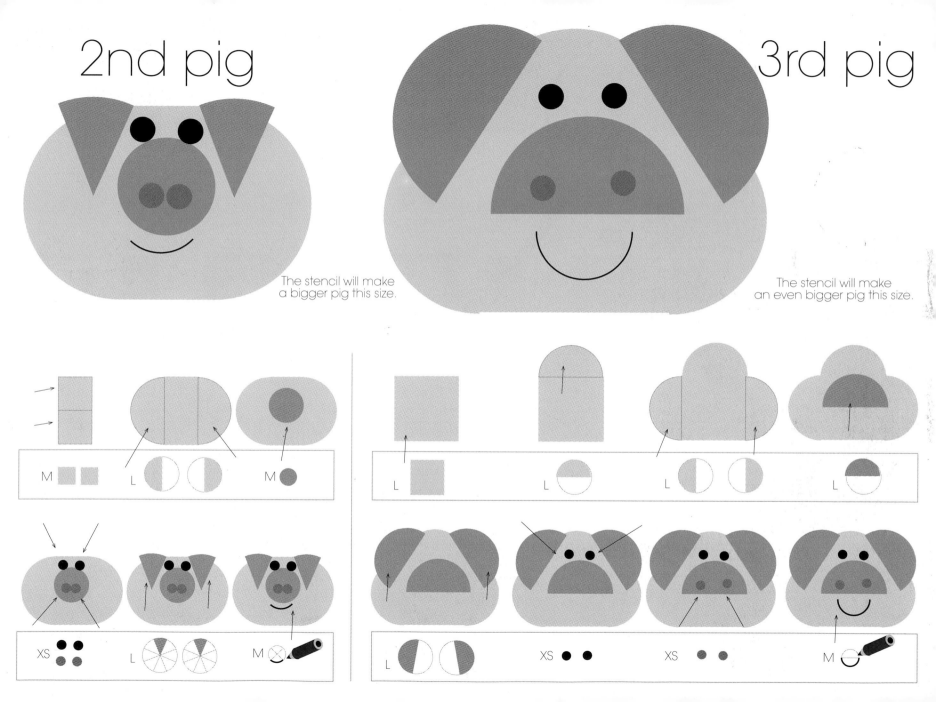

M

L   M

XS   L   M

L   L   L   L

L   XS   XS   M

engine

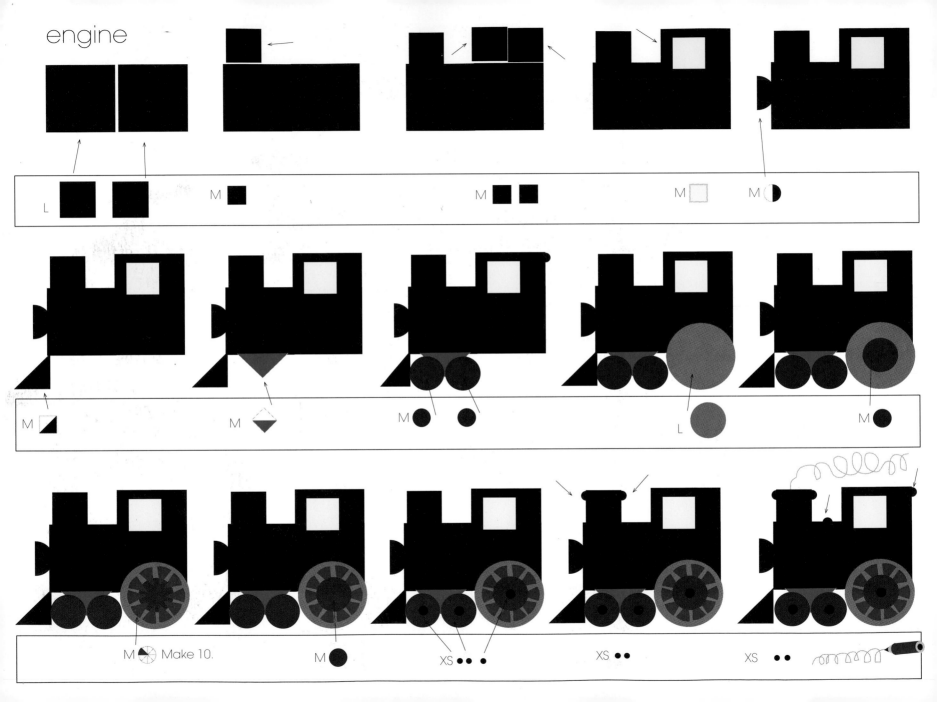

L

M

M

M

M

M

M

M

L

M

M Make 10.

M

XS ● ● ●

XS ● ●

XS ● ●

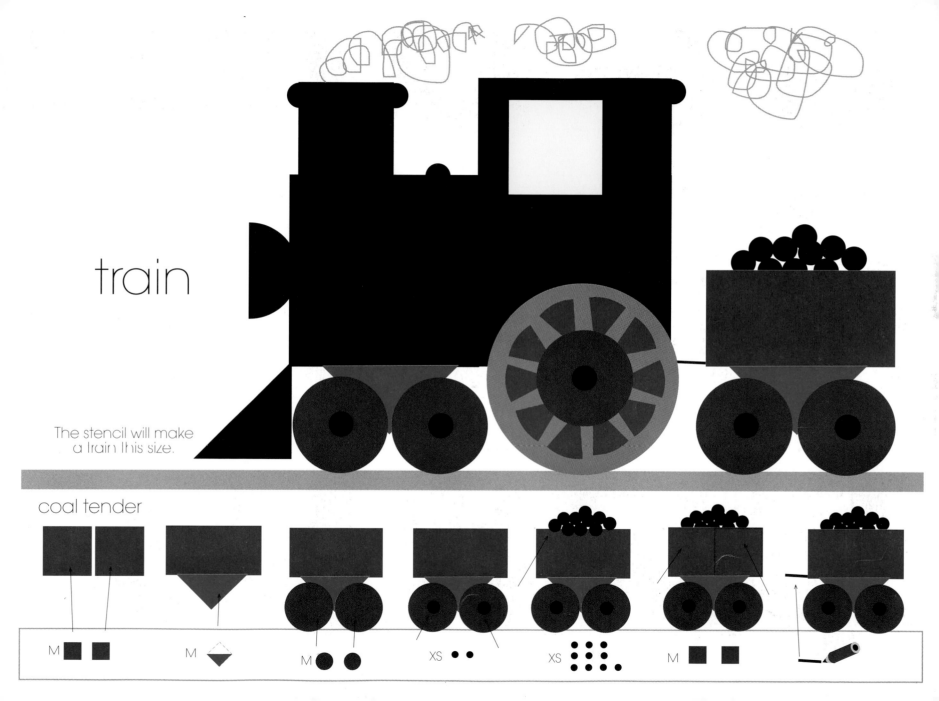

train

The stencil will make
a train this size.

coal tender

M ■ ■   M ◆   M ● ●   XS • •   XS ⦂⦂⦂   M ■ ■

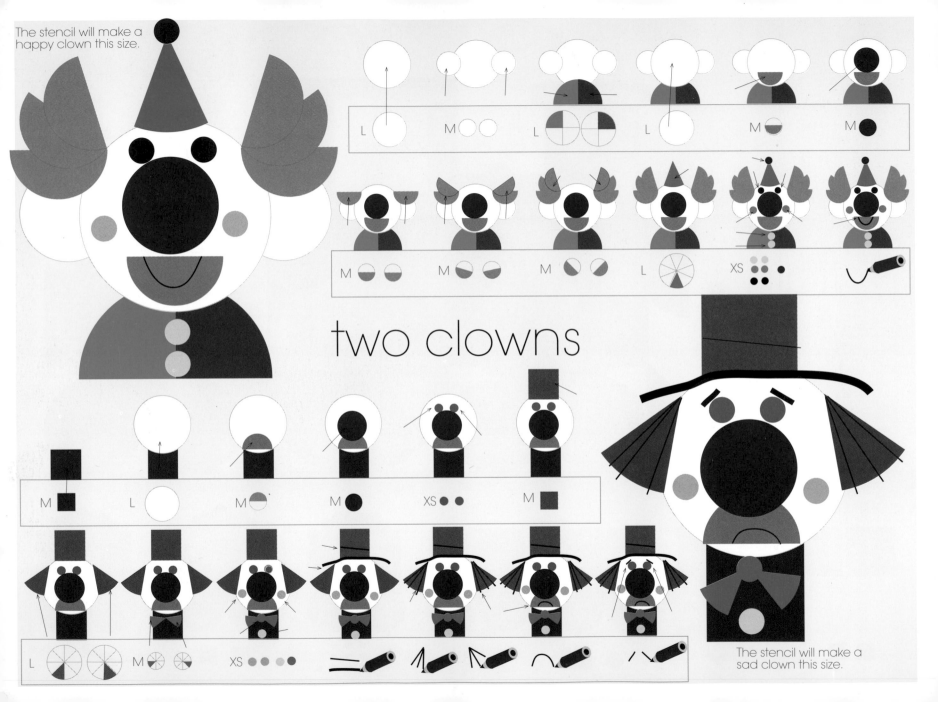

The stencil will make a happy clown this size.

two clowns

The stencil will make a sad clown this size.

L

M ○ ○

L

L

M

M

M ◐ ◐

M ◐ ◐

M ◑ ◑

L

XS

M ◐

L ○

M ◐

M ●

XS ● ●

M ▪

L

M

XS ● ● ● ●

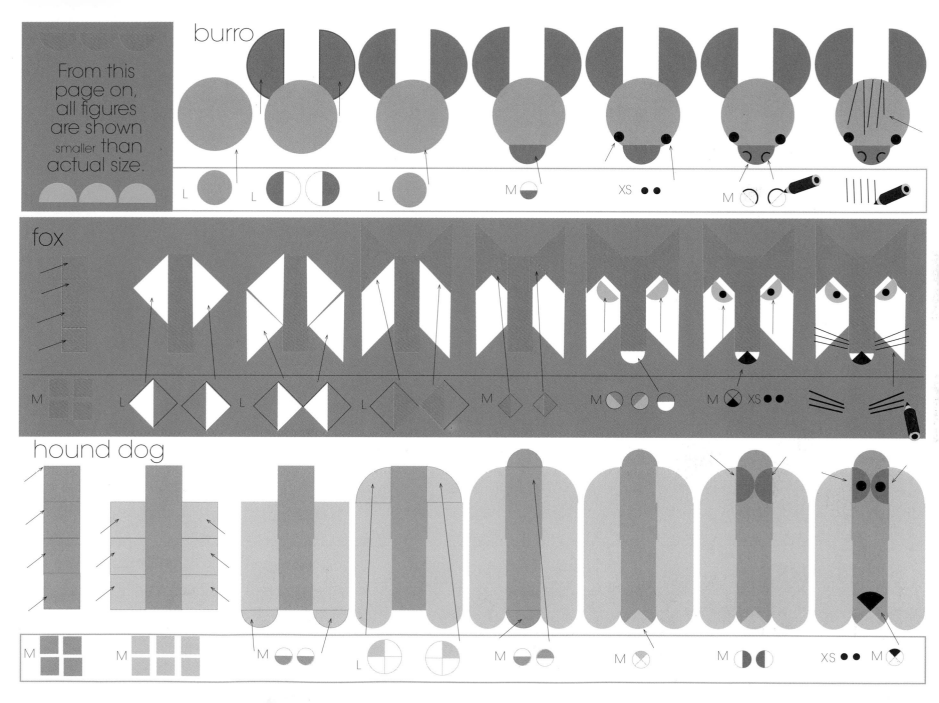

From this page on, all figures are shown smaller than actual size.

burro

L

L

L

M

XS ● ●

M

fox

M

L

L

M

M

M ⊗ XS ● ●

hound dog

M

M

M

L

M

M ⊗

M

XS ● ● M

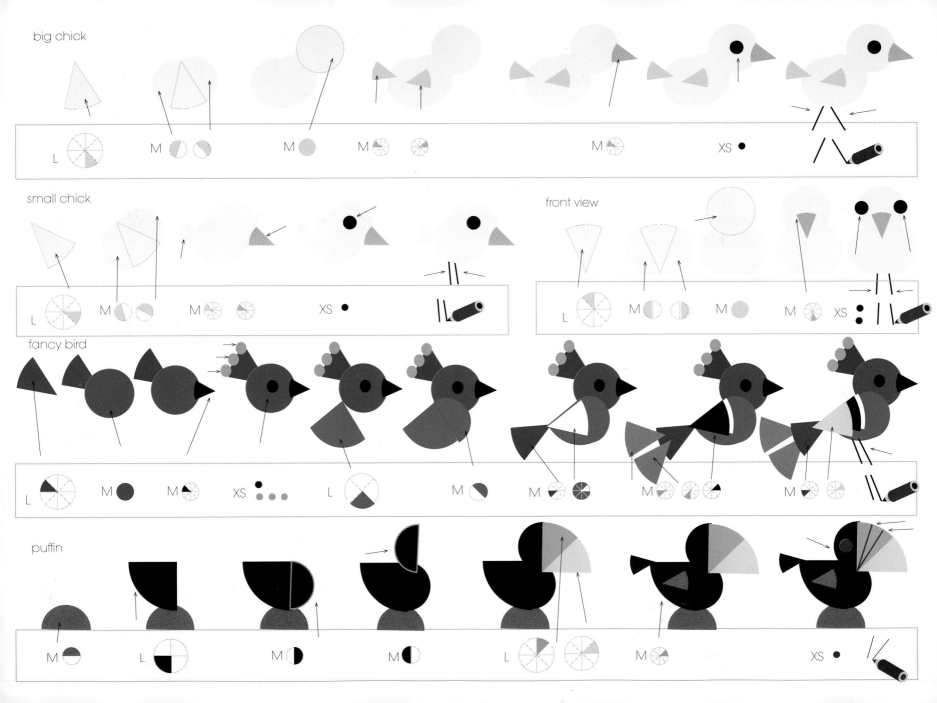

big chick

L M M M M XS

small chick

L M M XS

front view

L M M M XS

fancy bird

L M M XS L M M M M

puffin

M L M M L M XS

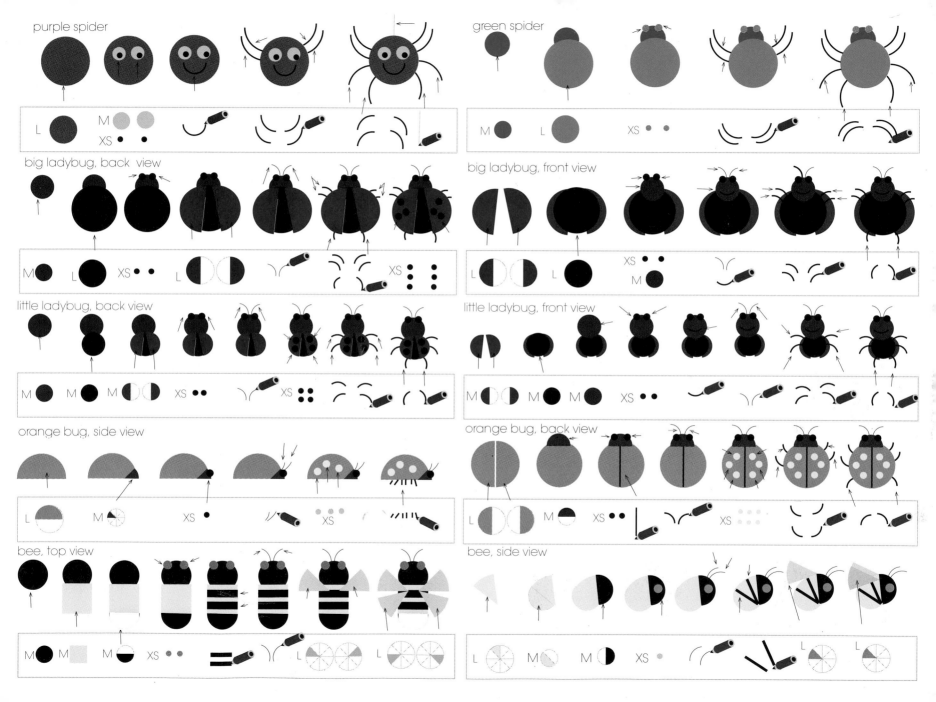

purple spider

green spider

big ladybug, back view

big ladybug, front view

little ladybug, back view

little ladybug, front view

orange bug, side view

orange bug, back view

bee, top view

bee, side view

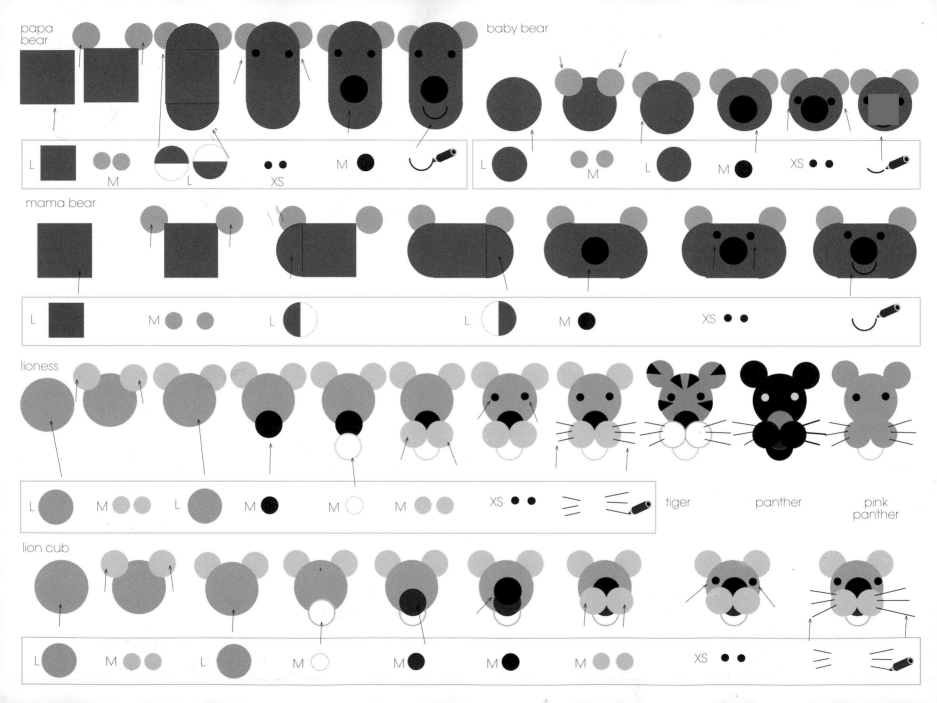

papa bear

baby bear

L   M   L   XS   M

L   M   L   M   XS

mama bear

L   M   L   L   M   XS

lioness

tiger   panther   pink panther

L   M   L   M   M   M   XS

lion cub

L   M   L   M   M   M   XS

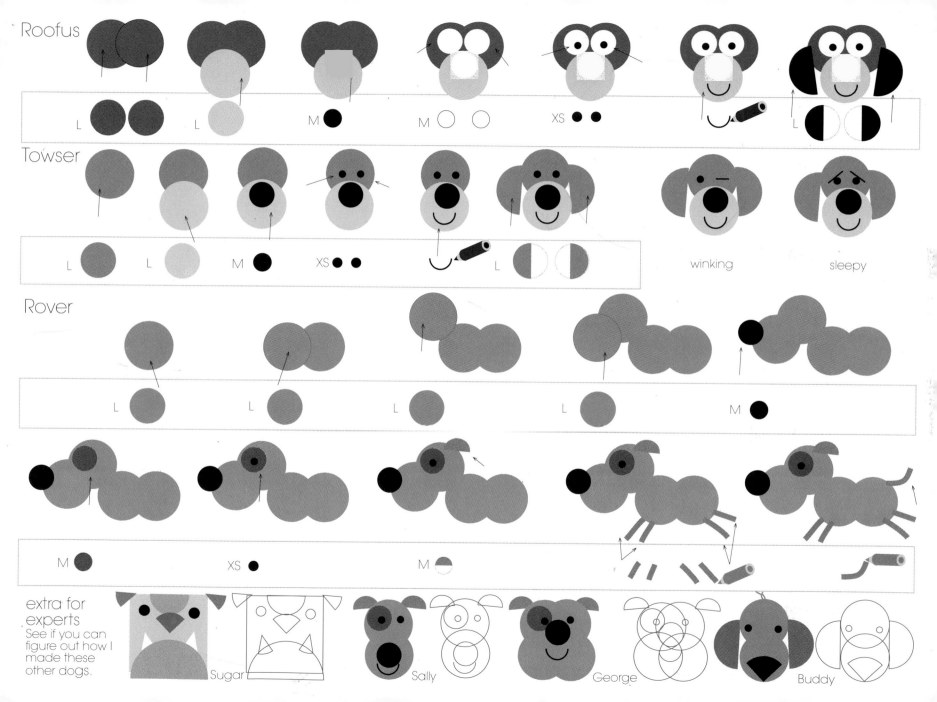

Roofus

L

L

M

M

XS

L

Towser

L

L

M

XS

L

winking

sleepy

Rover

L

L

L

L

M

M

XS

M

extra for
experts
See if you can
figure out how I
made these
other dogs.

Sugar

Sally

George

Buddy

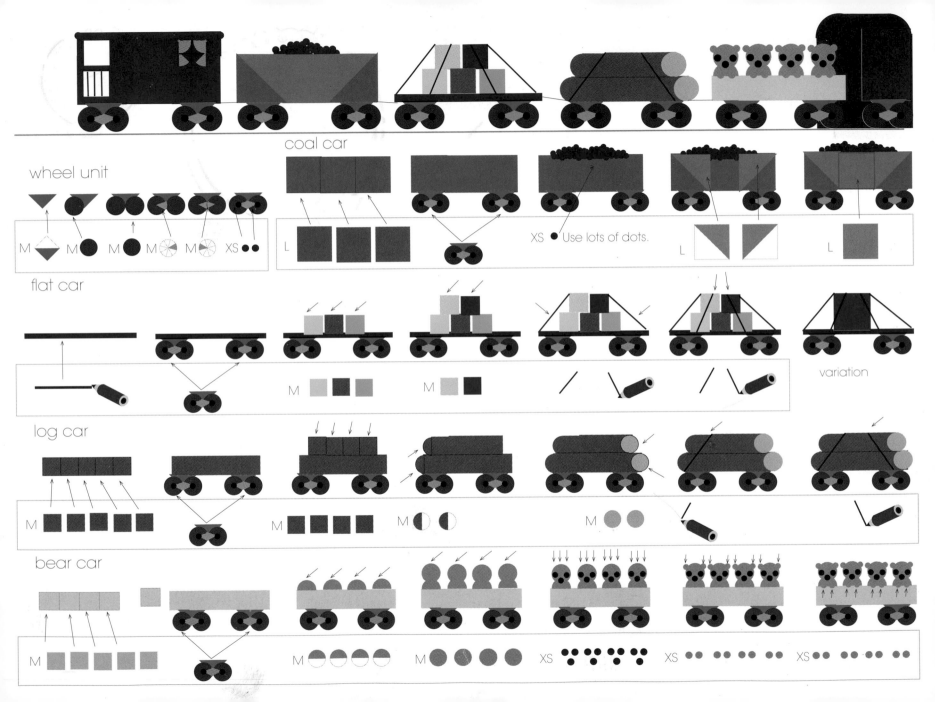

wheel unit

M ▽ / M ● / M ● / M ◉ / M ◉ / XS ●●

coal car

L [■ ■ ■] / XS ● Use lots of dots. / L [◣ ◣] / L ■

flat car

M [■ ■ ■] / M [■ ■] / variation

log car

M [■ ■ ■ ■ ■] / M [■ ■ ■ ■] / M ◖ ◗ / M ● ●

bear car

M [■ ■ ■ ■] / M ◖ ◗ ◖ ◗ / M ● ● ● ● / XS ●●●●●●●● / XS ● ● ● ● / XS ● ● ● ● ● ●

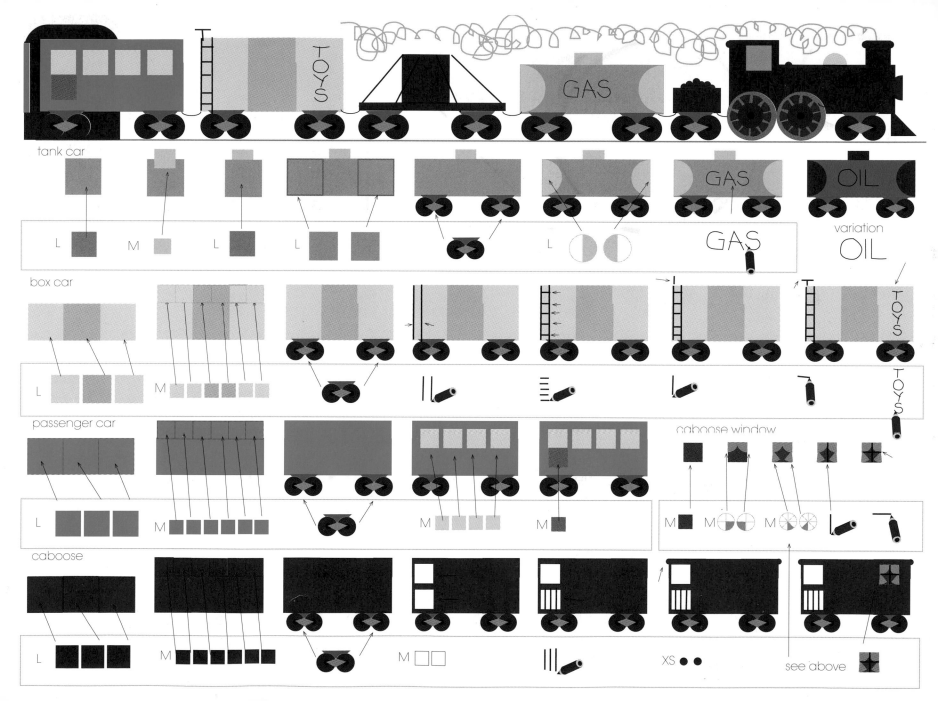

tank car

L   M   L   L   GAS

variation
OIL

box car

L   M

caboose window
M   M   M

passenger car

L   M   M

caboose

L   M   M □□   XS ● ●

see above

Combine letters, numbers, and pictures to make posters, signs, bulletin boards, and more.

OPEN

FRACTIONS

CAKE SALE

VISITORS 23
HOME 46

FRESH BAIT

Large (L) squares make letters this size.

Medium (M) squares make letters this size.

DEN 2

QUILTS

YARD SALE

Small (S) squares make letters this size.

To make letters with a more rounded appearance, use 1/4 circles, twice the size of the square, as corner units.

corner units

BASIC

M

ROUND CORNER

L

for inquiring minds

As you can see on this page, there are other ways to use Picture Pie pieces to make owls. There are also other cats, other dogs, other birds, other everything. Much has been left for you to explore and discover.

time saver

The XS circle is used in this book to make eyes and other small details. It is the same size (1/4" diameter) as a standard paper punch-out and a standard pencil eraser. Punching the eyes out of paper or stamping them using an eraser and a stamp pad will save you *a lot* of time.

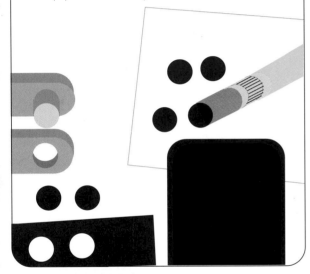

math connection

Picture Pie units are a full circle, 1/2, 1/4, 1/8 of a circle. a full square, and 1/2 of a square.
Fractions can be beautiful.

other methods

If you would like to use colored pencils or paint, you can still follow the instructions in this book. Just use the outline and fill-in method. Here's how:

colored pencils

1. Outline *all* shapes in the color you want them to be.

2. Fill in.

paint

1. Outline *all* shapes with pencil.

2. Outline shape with paint.

3. Fill in with paint.

other sizes

You can make any size set of Picture Pie pieces as long as you remember that the large (L) shapes are twice as big as the medium (M) shapes and that the medium (M) shapes are four times as large as the extra small (XS) shapes.

XS=1"	M=4"	M=4"	L=8"	L=8"

To make a custom set of Picture Pie pieces:

First cut a set of circles and squares out of paper.

To make two 1/2 circles, fold circle in half, crease, and cut.

To make two 1/4 circles, fold 1/2 circle in half, crease, and cut.

To make two 1/8 circles, fold 1/4 circle in half, crease, and cut.

To make two 1/2 squares, fold square in half diagonally, crease, and cut.

Use your paper patterns to make a set of cardboard shapes. Keep the cardboard shapes to use as templates.

USING THE STENCIL

Since small items such as stencils are easily misplaced, the Picture Pie stencil has been designed to remain part of the book. When you want to use it, just flip it out, and you will be able to see the stencil and any page in the book at the same time. When you are through, flip it back inside the book for safekeeping.

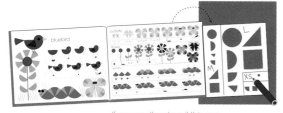

If you use the stencil this way, you should mark the XS, M, and L using the drawing on this page as a guide.

YOU CAN ALSO ...

Use the stencil to make a set of cardboard patterns and then draw around the patterns to make Picture Pie shapes.

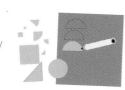

OR ...

Cut the stencil out of this book and cut it into as many pieces as you wish (if this is your book!).

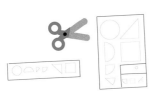

If stencil is lost or damaged, you can photocopy or trace this drawing to make a new one.

M

L

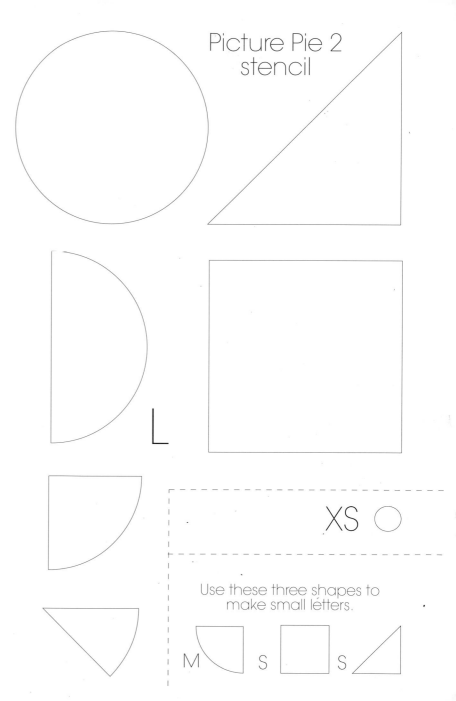

Picture Pie 2
stencil

XS ○

Use these three shapes to make small letters.

M S S

First Edition

ISBN 0-316-23458-3

Library of Congress Catalog Card Number 94-29064

10 9 8 7 6 5 4 3 2 1

Published simultaneously in Canada
by Little, Brown & Company (Canada) Limited

Printed in China

I have been using circles, rectangles, and triangles to make pictures since 1961. *The Wing on a Flea* was my first book on this subject; this is the seventeenth.

Every part of this book, from sketches to finished art, was created on a Macintosh 11ci computer using the programs Aldus FreeHand and Quark XPress. Because of its complexity, it would have been impossible for *me* to do it any other way. The type used is Adobe Avant Garde Extra Light.

If you would like to try a simpler version of the system presented in this book, look for the book *Picture Pie* at your favorite bookstore or library. It uses these five units ⟶  instead of the thirteen used in this book.